Abādi

Towards Eternal Life

Shaykh Fadhlalla Haeri

Abādi

Towards Eternal Life

Shaykh Fadhlalla Haeri

Zahra Publications

Zahra Publications

Published by Zahra Publications
www.shaykhfadhlallahaeri.com
info@shaykhfadhlallahaeri.com
www.zahrapublications.pub

© Shaykh Fadhlalla Haeri, 2025

All rights reserved. Except for brief quotations in critical articles or reviews, no part of this book may be reproduced in any manner without prior written permission from Zahra Publications.

Copying and redistribution of this book is strictly prohibited.
Designed and typeset in South Africa by Quintessence Publishing
Cover design adapted from the work of Mobeen Akhtar

Set in 10 points on 16 points, Myriad Pro
Printed and bound by Lightning Source

ISBN (Printed Version) — Paperback: 978-1-7764901-8-9

Foreword

It is in human nature to seek a perfect state where one is content, tranquil and joyful. Every human is made up of two entities, one is discernible and has evolved from the early inception of life culminating in animals and humans. The other is a mysterious soul that radiates life and creates what we consider as normal day-to-day living.

Each one of us contains the basic, selfish creature, as well as the pure light of the soul. We are on earth to practice, by conscious effort and grace, to be more attuned to the highest within us - the soul. In between, we make mistakes and learn in preparation for the next phase of life which is without the limitations of space and time. It is a participative destiny and we need to do the best we can by living in the moment and taking responsibility for our own actions and difficulties.

Abādi represents a state where the human side is illumined by the spirit within and resonates with the eternal boundlessness. All living beings are on the path towards Abādi, the ever perfect gardenic heavenly situation on earth.

Most living beings, especially human beings, are composed of two entities. One is a self-concerned animal evolving over time driven by the rise of consciousness and intelligence. The other is a divine force which produces life and its driving forces to ensure survival and continuity. A human being contains many of the animal traits and attributes. This is the dual nature of humanity.

The most important challenge in human life is the acceptance of death. When the end of life on earth is recognised as a transit to a higher zone of consciousness, our outlook and attitude towards every aspect of day-to-day life change radically. Then, life on earth is seen as a preparation for life after death at a higher zone of consciousness.

Abādi

I want to live longer.

Please don't ask how long

Life is eternal

You cannot cut it up into pieces

Limitations vanish within

the limitless

from where love and

generosity

emerge,

permeating

the whole cosmos.

Consciousness of time begins with birth and ends with death. Whoever manages to transcend time through stillness and silence may realise that death simply concludes earthly consciousness, whereas life continues eternally.

The desire to escape the bleak mundane to where there is constant joy and delight is a natural drive towards boundless consciousness. Eternity will be experienced fully after death.

At the gate of truth, you glimpse boundlessness and eternal pure consciousness.

Abadi

Life reveals numerous levels of beauty and grace, and sometimes, the darker side of light.

Judgment will affect the clarity of witnessing the reality of a situation.

Being fully present in the moment, action and inaction are in perfect balance.

The soul's origin is divine and ever perfect. The ego-self is its earthly shadow that connects through conditioned consciousness. Living creatures survive due to the light of the soul, whereas the ego longs for eternal life and its origin.

To live joyfully is to follow the way of nature with its unexpected changes and turns. The less we interfere with the natural flow of earthly life and creation, the greater we experience harmony and ease.

Life is most precious, a gift from the Creator. Our love for free gifts simply reflects the fact of the free gift of life.

Cause and effect mirror each other and sometimes exchange positions. A hero may be regarded as a cause of change, or as the outcome of change.

Feeling anxious or insecure is a reflection of the shadow self and conditioned consciousness drifting in time whilst bound in space.

Even when everything is good, there is still some subtle concern and uncertainty. You can only do your best and trust the rest.

A seeker thought that the sage calmed the storm, whereas in truth the sage simply shifted to where it was calm.

For short-term success, you need clear information and decisive action. As for long-term success, you need patience and regular reference to the constant and eternal. For lasting success, just remain in the eternal moment.

If you wish your action to be absolutely perfect, then simply do not act.

Time emerges from eternal timelessness, which is the origin and destiny of the soul. Time is the earthly womb of conditioned consciousness that prepares us for the hereafter and cosmic consciousness.

With reflection and silence, you may witness the vast universal connectedness and timelessness.

There is a touch of the perfect in every situation, which is revealed by pure witnessing when judgment stops.

Whenever you are really content, with no desires or hopes, you are in touch with the perfect present.

To be fully efficient, you need to be fully present in the moment now.

If you want a glimpse of eternity, lose time and space and all discernable consciousness.

If not troubled by a need, you are burdened by other concerns, uncertainties and fears. Time is a constant challenge for whoever is guided by a mind conditioned by changing space and time.

An observant visitor may enjoy the surprises and thrills of new surroundings more than the resident who has been there for a long time and has become too familiar with the same surroundings.

Much of what we do relates to prolonging or ending time or widening or shrinking space: the soul is eternally boundless.

To live longer

They prescribed

No coffee

No music

No perfume

I died instantly

whilst living forever

in the eternal joyful garden

where perfumed music carried

the grace of eternal light

radiating

life

eternally.

Intelligence reduces choice or alternatives, leading to one optimum choice at that instant.

Earthly consciousness is an early stage of awakening to the divine light of the soul, which will be fully experienced after death. The removal of ego-self illusions of individuality and separation reveals the effulgent cosmic light. Like what happens when the particle is experienced as a wave function.

The root of intelligence is like a beam that emanates from the Creator but appears modified within space and time.

The most valuable possession you have in life is life itself. With grace and reflection, you may realise the sacred nature of life, and that the body and mind are earthly. The shadow you is the housekeeper for your soul before its return to its heavenly home.

The newborn baby has little understanding or differentiation, but it eventually evolves to full comprehension and ego-discernment. With old age, awareness and discrimination begin to recede again until death. Life's journey is between the rise and a fall in earthly consciousness.

With frequent practice of silence and stillness, you may reach the gate of pure consciousness.

You may feel special, unique, unlike everyone else. Yet, you may also feel that others have a similar feeling, and that is disturbing - The way out of this conflict is the realization of the one cosmic Author of all.

The observers were eagerly asking, "Who is the winner?" Super-ego declares, "All are losers, except me. And in truth, I am also a passing shadow." All is due to the divine light.

Did they love me?

You were most adored by the Creator and a few creations. Life is the emergence of perfect love and a web of connections full of shadows and lights.

Each day is a new page in your biography, laid on top of the previous one. Each day links within the web of life's connections, seen and unseen.

It is always the same, appearing different. But after a while, maybe a thousand years, or when time stops, you glimpse the eternally present One, ever constant—always.

Uncertainty surrounds life; that is certain. Naturally, we always look for certainty. Truth is always there, ever bright behind shadows. That certainty is the source of all uncertainty.

Abādi

Truth declared, "Try as you might, it is all within my cosmic will, eternally One and boundless."

My ego-self cried, "If you leave again, I shall die!" Then my soul declared, "Life will continue, as it always has, whether you are dead or alive."

"I am right," everyone thinks. Sometimes they are right, and sometimes wrong. Life is between eternal perfection and apparent chaos.

Cornered with myself again. The resident ego deceiver, blaming others near and far. But no one can describe the nature of the receptive resident self, an ever changing shadow.

What you desire most now may become what you detest most later. Uncertainty is most reliable.

Living creatures are obsessed with life and fear death. Yet life is eternal, whilst death leads to another zone of consciousness.

Like you and others, I, too, looked at other paths
that promised salvation. One day, by Grace,
I realised there was no I. A real path points
towards losing self-illusions and identity. The
light of Reality is ever bright when you step out
of darkness.

Nirvana is beyond the darkness of duality and
the illusions of conditioned consciousness. Two
sets of births lead back to the Essence, eternally
present, but veiled to those who are in the
darkness of the ego-self.

Recognising the constantly changing, physical
and emotional states, is due to the constancy of
the light of the soul.

Now

I cried

I must help them

I cannot let them down

Even wailing

without tears

you expect the sound

As it is normal

they say

Part of the collective

deceptions and shadows

We are all

In it.

At the dawn of creation life radiated forth awakening matter to receive and express countless messages and forms. As life is eternal, so too is the inner soul and its light that shines through every manifestation. Life on earth is a natural transformation and involves the shift in the level of conscious awareness from a limited and conditional state of duality to a higher zone.

We need each other. Here and now. What about later? We need the bonds and connections to the original Oneness without separation or change in time. As it is in truth. Always.

To live with a kind and loving partner can increase dependency and fear of loss, as well as reduce the possibility of transcending duality to its origin of unity. But it is nice – for now.

Again and again, we make the same mistake because of loyalty to habit and constancy. Eternal sameness, highlighted by change.

Nature liberates plants from the confusion of choice and drives us out of the darkness of the self to the light of the soul and the path of eternity. Perfection of no choice.

Impatience is the dark side of the eternal soul, which is always in the now. Patience is grooming the earthly self to be like the soul that caused it.

They struggle to get there, but soon the hope for more benefits leads towards the next cycle of illusion, of achievement and progress. Thank God for death.

"I am angry!" she screamed. "And I blame everyone for that, including myself. I am not violent or vicious, but I am burning with anger, disappointment, regret, total frustration!" She began weeping for not living, fully, whilst still alive.

To participate, to anticipate, to hope, to follow desires and wishes – this is who we are. Partially awake to the eternal light, partially uncertain about the web of space and time that holds us.

Hope fades away without faith, trust or action. We hope the future will be better, but often it is illusive wishful thinking.

Happiness was promised and accepted. All earthly creatures hope for eternal happiness.

To judge, you may feel better, but it masks clarity of understanding and appropriate connection and action.

I realise my mistake now, but it is too late, and I am not the same as yesterday. Perpetual change is life's constant challenge which always wins whilst I lose.'

Whatever exists is touched by the Real, however short in space and time. The Real is boundless and eternal and leaves its traces throughout the universe. The Real is sacred and is the cause of all.

You are real and false all the time. So am I. And so is every living creature. Heavenly light floating amongst earthly shadows.

On rare occasions, life flows with perfect ease, perfect fit, with no resistance. Ease upon ease. When the ego-self is not interfering, the divine Reality is effulgent.

"I thought I was going mad," he said, "until I came to know they all are totally insane but deceive themselves to be normal."

The child played Superman. Now, a politician with a superego, he promises a better and happier life. Exhausted, after months of excitement, he wins the election. The morning of the inauguration, he faints on stage halfway through his speech. A fatal heart attack saves the people from his illusions and deceptions – for a while, at least.

In everything good there is a trace of bad, and in everything bad there is a touch of the good.

Death is much feared and causes much confusion and conflict. You don't like to die, yet you surely will die. But tell me, what is after death? It is here that fantasy plays absurd roles.

To avoid disappointments, just live fully in the light of eternal life's ever-present appointment.

I am very content and happy now. No needs, desires or hopes. I wish this lasts forever. Ever-present in the now, absent from past or future. Graced by amnesia of time due to the power of now.

Then the colour changed, a new smell emerged, before disappearing into the duality of consciousness and noise. Life's confusions are normal and stimulate awakening to the One.

Generosity in times of ease is a flow of kindness, and in times of hardship, it is a flow of Grace.

In the presence of others, you may attempt to look happy, despite your agitation. Your soul is ever-content, and that is what enables the ego-self to pretend.

Most living creatures prefer to take more and give less. The soul is in a state of boundless goodness.

Being kind and duty-bound, I naturally was pleased with myself. A welcome trap that can become deadly, with no way out. Unless you lose the trap of self and its related illusions.

Wealth and power may satisfy a few desires, but they also produce new fears and uncertainties.

To experience magic or witness a miracle is a natural desire in us, encouraged by the miracle of life itself.

With the least desires or needs, the ego-self is dormant. Then you invent needs for others' sake, and the chain of action and reaction trips you up, and distractions trap you.

They were competing to see who owns more, but no one asked, who owns you, or who are you?

He said, "I didn't do it. It fell and broke. It's the truth." The lie is the dark side of truth. Like all that exists, it emerged from the infinite and boundless, appearing for a while as partially true.

At the end of the week-long Himalayan retreat, they lined up to thank the Swami for showing them the truth. Greeting them he said, "No one could show the truth; in truth, there is only the truth. You can point at the dark veils that cover the truth. It is by turning away from the darkness that you face light."

Who did it? Bring the culprit to justice. We are the keepers of balance; justice must prevail, mostly as seen or witnessed, or even imagined. But we must apply justice. God knows best, and we can only punish the identity that appears real.

Anxiety, fears and concerns will vanish when you know that all events and appearances follow the pattern of perfect order, ever-changing whilst emerging from the constant.

To do your best every moment reflects the ever-present perfect moment.

From eternal perfection, every moment appears, with different signals suitable for the receiver.

A story is complete when it ends, so the meaning and purpose of life will be clear after death.

The spring is ending, they said. No one could explain what the beginning or the end is. Whereas everyone is living between a past and present, with some concern about the future. Endless cycles within time and space.

No one is really here; no one is truly present, for no one is free of space or time. The eternal light will show itself again when all else has disappeared.

To touch the light of cosmic Oneness,

lose yourself.

The more completely,

the better.

Then you may catch a glimpse of the

original and eternal Source.

The less of the so called 'you'

the clearer Reality shows itself.

The child wondered, "What use are books, schooling or teachers?" With maturity, it is realised that books are helpful for skills and wisdom, for better judgment and less suffering. A partial but helpful answer.

Within the field of duality, learning skills can be transferred and taught, but with higher knowledge, closer to the original Oneness, you need to stop all references and rationality. Be in the now.

With success in school came vanity. But all was modified by life's challenges, and the truth was revealed with the practice of silence and presence. When all distractions vanish, truth shines above.

The hero is dead now. The heirs are left with a chest full of medals and memorabilia. Each one has a different opinion on what to do in order to keep the memory alive. Years later, the offspring simply ignored the chest of medals, and in time, all was forgotten.

Love is a powerful drive in consciousness which gets restricted when objectified. Timelessness and boundlessness are necessary for love to flourish and be durable. Thriving love is like a healthy, growing tree, with many branches and limbs. When love is confined and conditioned, it withers and dies.

Most humans consider death as an enemy rather than a friend. Fear of death precedes death because one has not experienced joyful submission to life's perfect unfoldments.

The relentless drive to know yourself is from your own soul within your heart. It illumines its shadow ego, which enables it to connect with the earthly realities through conditioned consciousness.

"Do you still love me?" she asked again. "I feel lonely, insecure and unsafe, just as the astrologer predicted." Then she began sobbing. "It always happens like this, and it's all beyond me, as everything in life is beyond me.". After a while, she became quiet, and said, "The real issue is that I don't know who I am."

The truth is that there is no reliable constant you, except for your soul. Your ego-self is ever-changing, admitting its shadowy reality.

The real you can only be seen through the ever-changing impressions gained by consciousness, the ever-changing emerging from the ever-constant.

The endless question as to who I am will disappear with the light of the spirit, which is effulgent and constant and overcomes the shadow-self or ego. Seperateness and identity is a shadow that vanishes in the light of Reality.

Every living entity has some anxiety to maintain life for longer, whereas life itself is eternal. For a while, the body and mind host the soul, which leaves its short journey in the field of earthly duality.

Everyone is challenged by space and time. The inner light occasionally shows the transience of it all. Everything exists for a moment, then vanishes. Its illusory existence is a prelude to another phase of consciousness after death.

Mercy and grace permeate everything all the time, including sight and insight. This becomes clearer if you are neutral and accept pain and pleasure. A greater gift is to accept uncertainty at all times and situations, including what you had considered to be sure.

Colours and smells appear and disappear. Earthly life is all about emergence and submergence.

The inner voice was clear and commanding – be still, be silent, be present. From before time to beyond the end of time. Truth engulfs all that exists; known and unknown.

You long to belong, you also long to be unique and special. You desire to be respected and distinguished, but sometimes you also like to be anonymous. You love to be the best, and yet you know your limitations and shortcomings. There lies the problem. There, too, is the solution, when you discover the soul within.

The fellow said, "Give me the end of the story first, and then start at the beginning. When you read the end first, the beginning will fit better, and you will remain in the moment and present."

People get stuck where they are because they like what they are familiar with. It gives the illusion of continuity and foreverness.

In every symmetry there is a hint of asymmetry, and in every asymmetry, there is a touch of symmetry.

Planet Earth is a physical nursery for consciousness to evolve and intelligence to rise from defined limitations toward the boundless. We are being prepared for a magnificent, eternal and boundless zone of consciousness.

The natural human drive towards higher consciousness requires one to enter the intermediate zone of stillness, silence and serenity. In that state opposites reconcile and dualities yield into unity. Every action dissolves every atom into its role in the cosmic rhythm of wholesomeness.

Expectations and hopes are drives for a better future. The ultimate future is another zone of consciousness beyond the duality of space and time.

The optimum state of consciousness and spiritual intelligence is reached when death is regarded as a natural and welcome next stage in the evolution of consciousness.

"I've made it," she thought. "Just look at the photos to confirm it. But now I want everything to stop, because I fear what comes next. I pray to God to stop time so that I remain on top forever."

Abādi

Within conditioned consciousness, no one attains reliable certainty and security because life is experienced as change within space and time. Full consciousness is experienced after death when the shadowy ego-self veil is removed.

When you are aware of the ego-self and the infinite play of dualities, you may recognise the changing shadows and temptations. I owe much to my ego-self, for I can now focus upon the light that illumines temporary consciousness.

Being prepared for life after death will help you to have a fulfilled life before death.

Life's experiences become most special when you have no expectations or judgements, just witnessing events flowing in their natural way. This is witnessing perfection.

You strive for better performance and outcome, but ultimately, all earthly deceptions will end. Only through stillness, silence and presence, you catch a glimpse of the eternal presence.

Most people welcome gifts and presents. A few have risen to prefer giving to receiving. Their cups are overflowing. Few are above the good and bad of movement and change.

Abādi

Whatever exists, is touched by cosmic love. Adored by its Creator, it expresses its presence add radiate aspects of the miracle.

The sage said, "Just remember that we are all within the divine deception. Separation and identities are experienced within the field of dualities originated by divine unity."

Human life is experienced within conditioned consciousness and is characterised by uncertainty and vagueness – that is how divine unity illuminates ego and vanity.

What you see and discern is a minute fraction of what there is in creation what there is in creation which is endless.

Human consciousness on earth is within dualities and drives every individual to seek a friend or partner who can serve as a mirror to confirm unity. In essence, spiritual mirrors reflect cosmic Oneness.

All intentions and actions contain a strand that naturally connects and links to the original cosmic Oneness.

Conditioned consciousness and dualities on earth can help to discover Oneness. Every living creature loves itself the most, and every self loves eternal life. All other considerations and drives are secondary to self-love and the obsession with life and Oneness.

When you witness life through the lens of your own soul, events that normally cause anxiety, fear and sorrow will simply be regarded as agreeable or disagreeable events, by treating them as simple facts.

The natural inclination towards a better future propel us towards the light of the soul, which is ever perfect.

Uncertainty and insecurity propel us to a better future. The soul drives us towards a higher self and the next state of consciousness.

We expect a benefit in whatever we do, whilst the soul is beyond any gain or loss.

Truth reveals itself whenever and however with different levels of clarity.

I promised

as usual

without a thought

don't ask why

I never know

Nor do I want to know

For

as usual

It is not always useful

to know

why.

If you manage to put yourself fully in someone else's position, physically and emotionally, then you would do exactly as they do.

It is human nature to share with others what is considered beautiful, desirable or admirable, and it is our nature to cover or conceal what is not. We seek perfection - a reflection of the divine soul within.

Disappointments are due to inappropriate expectations; indeed, most expectations cause some concern and uncertainty.

Sometimes a living creature considers itself to be very special or favoured. That is because of the soul within, providing life most special.

To be fully present in the moment, you need to step aside from the ego-self. To be fully aware of the eternal light of the divine, you need to be at one with your divine soul within.

Those who are partially awake, may experience some loneliness and alienation. With grace, they can accept that life on earth is work in progress. Life is eternal and is governed by a perfect Creator in every situation. Therefore, we are driven towards perfection.

Most people live their lives as sleepwalkers responding to shadows, dreams and nightmares.

Human life on earth is like being in a general hospital with numerous rehab sections. The healing process will lead to emergence from false identity and other illusions. The so-called 'you' has only a partial connection with the eternal and permanent soul within you, which will become fully clear upon death, when all veils are lifted.

Frequent awareness of the sublime soul and its perfect governance overrides anxieties, fears and sorrows.

Whatever is alive carries within it a memory of before time before time and the emergence of consciousness and life..

Good and bad, vices and virtues, attraction and repulsion, and all other dualities only exist within space and time.

Anything that exists is an aspect of duality and has emerged from its origin of unity with higher intelligence.

You think you know what to do, and you don't like to be told what to do by anyone else but yourself: an illusory trap. The idea of freedom of choice is due to the ego-self that can often bring suffering.

Life's experience leads to an obsession with personal life and the fear of losing it. Life, however, is eternal, and when we experience its perfect ways and governance in all situations and all times, our fears and desires may vanish. With perfect presence, lasting security and contentment prevails.

The desire to discover, explore, connect and be at one with creation ultimately leads us to be at one with the original, singular Source from which everything had emerged.

For most humans, fulfilment in life requires a loving partner, who is preferred over oneself and paves the way to reconnect with the original Oneness from which creation has emerged.

For a couple to enjoy a relationship, it must be based on harmony and complementarity. They must maintain respect for each other, as well as the desire to help and serve each other, whilst remembering that all have emerged from one Source. All souls are similar. Differences arise from the shadow-self, which is necessary for life on Earth. Differentiated sameness is the rule.

Normal connections and friendships with others may distract from the state of perfect presence and the light of Oneness.

To live with others in harmony and ease is natural when you live with constant reference to your own soul.

To forgive and forget is mostly for one's own sake. To be accountable and just is for everyone's sake as well as yours.

You are unlikely to find the One without the other. And with the other, you remain confused in the land of dualities with no lasting clarity.

To find what you want in time, you need to calibrate with that which is beyond time. To understand the self, you need the light of the soul.

The human being is born in time, and after death will experience timelessness.

Time flows with ease at a harmonious pace, unless you are in dis-ease.

Out-of-time experiences can be short or long as they are not emerging from time itself.

Every living creature is born in time, grows up in time and leaves time back to timelessness.

Time is the most valuable asset you have on earth, as it is limited and exhaustible. Your soul, however, is not limited by time or space.

Human love and respect for time is a reflection of the real reverence for what is eternal.

Our love for good health, longevity and wealth are part of our attempt to achieve ongoingness and the everlasting.

The more time has elapsed, the more stable the situation appears to be, and the more perspective changes.

After a good sleep, you wake up refreshed, enjoying the light of consciousness. After death, we experience a higher state of awakening, without the barriers of body, mind or emotions and the confinement of space or time.

Within our earthly consciousness, there is nothing that is absolutely reliable, for everything is an approximation of the real, including yourself.

Anything that exists in our world is an aspect of duality and becomes more stable with reference to the unifying field from which it emerged.

Participative destiny comes with immense responsibility. Whatever has been touched by divine life interacts and relates to other existences. When will is exercised the living entity participates in its destiny. Whoever realizes this truth will treat every action and thought with great respect and caution. No living being is excluded from this upward flow.

We live in a field of constant change and uncertainty. As such, it is not possible to experience, for any length of time or space, constancy or durability.

Our earthly conditioned consciousness is within a field that is constantly disturbed and uncertain. The changes can be local or universal. A slight disturbance in the ambient temperature will have repercussions that can ultimately have a major impact on life.

The inner state will become clearer when the outer fades. Then it may lead to the chain of deceptions of time and space, declaring the eternal truth is always before, after and within all.

The ego-self is a shadow of the soul, and as such, it is most elusive, as it has no sustainable reality.

A child accepts and rejects according to what pleases its emerging ego self. The young one adds consideration for others' views. A mature and wise person acts with kindness and consideration to others. The enlightened one enjoys the prevailing perfection at all time and places.

A beam of light produces many shadows, acknowledging the light itself.

Earthly confidence may lead to spiritual arrogance. True humility and loss of self lead to the door of spiritual awakening.

The desire for freedom of choice enables us to benefit from applying our intelligence and judgment. Correct choices will enable intelligence to rise and consciousness to flourish.

Reason and comprehension are early indicators of the light of intelligence. At its peak, intelligence shines to reveal cosmic Oneness.

When you have attained it all, you are also at the point of cheerful willingness to lose it all.

If happiness depends on any factor beyond yourself, it also brings insecurity and fear.

Honesty will eventually lead to the realisation that your identity is a short-term manifestation of a boundless, eternal Reality that contains all known and unknown.

Life is a free gift maintained by gratitude and accountable good conduct.

To be alive and well with no anxieties, fears, or sorrow is the foundation for happiness and joy and being with one's soul.

Cognizant and duty-bound, I was pleased with myself and walked into a new, dreadful trap of smugness.

Deadly, with no way out. Out of the trap, there is no self.

Human control is easiest in limited space and within a short time. You can easily move a finger, but not the branch of a tree far away.

Pride is a colour of life, the ultimate treasure. To attribute life to self is the opposite of truth. To celebrate life in gratitude is a joy that reflects divine grace.

The quality of the human experience on earth is a prelude to the next level of consciousness, which may manifest as between hell or paradise in the hereafter.

To be able to tap into boundless joy at any time and in any situation is a pinnacle of grace, which is the result of transcending the ego-self to its original soul. Full human potential is realised when the inner spiritual light illumines the shadows and uncertainties of day-to-day consciousness.

The path of awakening traverses unexpected terrains, including being deceived and pleased with one's progress out of darkness. You like to be favoured and regarded as special. Whatever exists is special and unique in its own way.

With limited opportunities and little prospect of a better future, life becomes dreary and bleak. One way out of this is through spiritual insights, which relate to the next zone of higher consciousness and life after death.

The natural human quest for happiness will eventually take the reflective seeker to a point of consciousness beyond duality, to the zone of light, spirits and the unseen.

To arrive at the state of witnessing perfection, desires and actions need to end.

In normal day-to-day interactions hope, belief and expectation are important ingredients, even though one experiences disappointments and pain. We are naturally inclined to believe and trust in goodness and a better future that is the life of the soul.

The purpose of life is to interact, make mistakes, suffer, cry, love and hope, for intelligence to rise to its origin – the soul, which is without shadows.

Human evolution tames the wildness in human life as a prelude to higher consciousness and spiritual intelligence that leads to the divine Source - boundless and eternal.

I am busy, please go away, but come back soon, bearing a gift, for I love presents. Perpetual life is the ultimate gift and present; like the eternal moment, it's always there, boundless in space and time. And now this is a present for you.

He was wafer-thin when we met. His nourishment was by smell or mere sight. Some called it homoeopathic food. Then he died, leaving me a note that read, "All of creation appears and disappears as cycles and vibrations, revealing eternal presence which I lived by in unity eternally."

You are temporary, but from a permanent state before time.

Every human being is composed of two different entities. One is an evolving animal creature limited to space and time. The other is a spiritual entity, which enables one to experience life. As spirits, we are all the same, and as creatures, we are always different.

With old age, most people become concerned with issues of health and death. With special experiences such as out-of-body or near-death experiences death is regarded as a change in consciousness and a liberation from the limitations of time and space. Therefore, very few beings regard death as the soul's liberation from the uncertainty of duality, a welcome natural experience.

Real contentment and peace are all attained when you know the perfection and generosity of the unique divine Author of all existential events and situations. All is ever perfect. All is from the perfect Author.

Generosity and kindness to others reduce self-concern and ego demands, thereby making it easier to experience higher consciousness and the eternal soul.

Our natural desire to share any goodness or special experience with someone else acknowledges the nature of the duality of consciousness on earth. This is the cause of looking for a soul mate

What is unknown is immense, and knowledge reveals only a small strand of it. Like daylight, knowledge sheds light on the surface of existence, yet much of creation remains hidden.

Conditioned consciousness seeks the unusual, something different from the norm, to expand its horizon. Pushing boundaries is a natural drive; it reflects the boundless nature of the soul.

It was here; I saw it. Now it is neither here nor there. I don't see it. The trick of space and time framing events to reinforce the illusion of separation and differentiation. The I that witnesses a glimpse of Truth that was the cause of the I in the first place.

This, too, will change. It will end, or pass. Like all events, creation expresses aspects of the Creator. The whole universe flashes aspects of the Creator - vast and eternal.

Patience, forbearance, forgiveness and all other virtues, as well as all vices, lose their meaning outside the boundaries of space and time, and whatever remains is Truth, untarnished.

Truth or reality is the most powerful force in existence and is masked by numerous filters, shadows and nets before it appears to human consciousness. Therefore, whatever we experience has a touch of truth. With the rise of consciousness and intelligence, we transcend some of the illusions and deceptions that veil the light of truth. When the ego-self is fully transcended by death. The light of the eternal soul shines effulgent with truth.

At the temple of truth

you only hear one litany

in all languages

including silence

with one meaning,

ever perfect.

The rise in intelligence and consciousnes may reduce

may reduce human suffering

and darkness.

The desire to believe can also cause darkness and suffering as does the hope for attaining what is desirable.

A politician may promise wealth and prosperity but often brings about great suffering, poverty and disappointments.

Human life on earth enables everyone to participate in their destiny as the outcome of their activity. Everyone is included in experiencing the results of their striving.

You may not like something, and yet it is the best for you. Also, you may desire something, and it is the worst for you.

Desires can confuse clarity and proper understanding, and not unless you are clear of all emotions and expectations will you see things for what they are.

Worldly success and wealth are often accompanied by other failures and impoverishment, which will be fully realised in the hereafter.

To be a good and proper witness, judge a situation, then stop. Then look at it again without your own opinion. Now you can witness.

It is a very popular reflection to ask whether the future is determined or changeable. The patterns of how things link and bring about an outcome do not change. What changes is what is applicable in your path of activity. The future changes if you change your attitude and direction.

When you attribute events to the maker or God, the story becomes very different to that when you think that you are the doer.

A human being is a sacred bundle of energy waves masquerading as an entity with an identity, coupled with the illusion of choice. Natural events sometimes appear slow. A mountain rises a few centimetres each year. On the other hand, the speed of light is three hundred thousand kilometres per second.

Before space and time appeared, there was only Oneness or singularity, and heaven and earth were seamlessly connected. Eternity is the nature of our soul or spirit and is glimpsed when touched by a special moment beyond time.

The practice of regular stillness and silence can lead to glimpses of perfection in every event or situation in life, irrespective of one's personal and emotional view. Whatever occurs is due to multiple interlinks between different entities, all of whom follow a perfect pattern, seen or unseen. This is witnessing perfection.

www.ingramcontent.com/pod-product-compliance
Lightning Source LLC
Chambersburg PA
CBHW060211050426
42446CB00013B/3047